Patience
Perseverance Through the Wait

Terri Ann Johnson

To a Tee Publishing
Washington, D. C.

This book is a work of nonfiction. These accounts are from the author's perspective and memories, and as such, are represented as accurately and faithfully as possible. To maintain the anonymity of the individuals involved, some of the names and details have been changed.

Patience: Persevering Through the Wait
Copyright © 2021 by To a Tee Publishing All rights reserved.

Edited by J. L. Campbell: jlcampbellwrites@gmail.com
Cover Designed by J. L Woodson: www.woodsoncreativestudio.com
Interior Designed by Lissa Woodson: www.naleighnakai.com
Beta: D. J. Mitchell

ISBN 978-1-7373562-0-2 (trade paperback)
ISBN 978-1-7373562-1-9 (eBook)

Without limiting the rights under copyright reserved above, no part of this publication may be reproduced, stored in, or introduced into a retrieval system, or transmitted, in any form, or by any means (electronic, mechanical, photocopying, recording, or otherwise) without the express written permission of both the copyright owner and the publisher of this book, except in the case of brief quotations embodied in critical articles and reviews.

For permission, contact Terri A. Johnson at terrijohnson419@gmail.com
To a Tee Publishing
Washington, D.C.
www.terriannjohnson.com

The scanning, uploading, and distribution of this book via the Internet or via any other means without the permission of the owner is illegal and punishable by law. Please purchase only authorized electronic editions and do not participate in or encourage electronic piracy of copyrighted materials. Your support of the author's rights is appreciated.

If you purchase this book without a cover, you should be aware that this book is stolen property. It is reported as "unsold and destroyed" to the publisher, and neither the author nor the publisher has received any payment for this "stripped" book.

Scripture quotations marked NIV are taken from the Holy Bible, New International Version®, NIV®. Copyright © 1973, 1978, 1984, 2011 by Biblica, Inc.™ Used by permission of Zondervan. All rights reserved worldwide. www.zondervan.com. The "NIV" and "New International Version" are trademarks registered in the United States Patent and Trademark Office by Biblica, Inc.™

♦ DEDICATION ♦

I dedicate this book to the memory of Mari-Christine Hart-Wright and Brian Roberts for showing me how to persevere through the peaks and valleys of the adoption process. You never gave up. Instead, you embraced the good times and endured the hard ones with grace and class.
Continue to rest in peace.

Until we meet again ...

♦ ACKNOWLEDGEMENTS ♦

First and foremost, I want to thank God for giving me the gifts of life, love, family, health, and our Lord and Savior Jesus Christ. Without these gifts nothing would be possible.

To my mom, dad, sister, and brother-in-law, who help me when I'm in the writing cave. And thank you for understanding that the hustle don't stop.

To my son, Joshua, who accepted eating more fast food than he should've while we were quarantined, and Mommy needed to write. Most of all, thank you for loving me in the midst of it all.

To my nieces and nephews, Krystal, Phillip, Jr., Christopher, Jr., and Naomi, who always step up when I need you to spend time with your cousin. We love you!

To Thelma Harris Johnson, Latreece Johnson Wade, and Rhonda Pope Brown, who helped me proofread and edit, thank you.

To the Zoom writing crew, thank you for setting time aside, daily, to fulfill our dreams.

To my editor, J.L. Campbell, for challenging me to improve the novel.

To D. J. Mitchell, the best beta reader this side of Jordan. Thank you for your comments and corrections.

Thank you to Naleighna Kai and to NK's Tribe Called Success for the accountability and motivation to keep going.

To J.L. Woodson, thank you for the awesome cover. Your work is phenomenal.

To Shawn Williams, for giving us the word to move this project forward.

To every reader and book club, thank you for your support. I hope you enjoy my first non-fiction work.

Terri Ann Johnson

Brand new shoes and sleepers never worn. After a while, family and friends forget the name, but you don't. Birthdays come and go and you still dream of milestones never met. Standing in a river of tears with an empty basket, the prayer is the same. Motherhood is a ministry. Why not me?

The silence can be deafening when prayers appear to go unanswered. Twin sins of fear and doubt close around her in sickening waves. A chasm grows where a child should be. Time winds down on a clock unseen and she folds her hands to pray.

Cradling him close, she counts fingers and toes as it dawns on her. Some answers require a lifetime of questions. Babies and dreams are no different.

Stephanie M. Freeman, author of *Necessary Evil* and *Unfinished Business*

Chapter 1
The Decision

As a little girl, I never imagined this would be my life.

Nothing or no one could've convinced me that the intricate fairytale I'd imagined for myself wasn't going to end with a husband and 2.5 children, at least one of whom would be graduating college while the mister and I planned romantic getaways from the joyfully rambunctious little ones who remained at home. Halfway through my 30's, marriage constantly buzzed through my mind. Subconsciously, I was drawn to men who didn't care a thing about commitment or could bring themselves to declare "I do" in front of God because the Lord would know they'd be lying. My romantic mishaps aren't exactly for these pages, however. We'll save those emotional expenditures for the next book.

Back to the fairytale.

When I tell you, I sifted through piles of wedding gowns in search of the perfect one to satisfy my hunger for marriage, it was almost like gluttony! There were so many styles I adored, but the ones with the sheer tops were my favorite. Once I settled on the style that suited my tastes the most, there were so many more decisions to be made. Should I choose white or off-white? Would I have a destination wedding, or host the ceremony at the Nation's Capital? Should the mani match the pedi? I meticulously planned the whole thing out, leaving no bouquet unturned. There was only one piece missing…the groom.

It wasn't long before the soundtrack I wrote to go along with my fairytale didn't make any sense: There was no ring, no dress, not even a single prospect whose proposal I'd accept or reject. I get it, the groom is probably a crucial part of the equation; however, did the fact that I didn't have one yet have to obliterate my entire dream? They make movies about those kinds of situations. I didn't want to live it, though.

In Jeremiah 29:11 God states, "For I know the plans I have for you…" Our heavenly Father does things His way to let us know He's in control.

Sometimes we can desire something so badly that we lose sight that there could be something bigger waiting for us. That was me. Caught between mourning my dreams, and still praying for them to manifest, when a soft voice tickled my ears. "Marriage might not be on the horizon, but I have other plans for you."

My mind was about to be blown by the plans God really had!

In the African American community, the word *adoption* tends to carry a negative connotation. Tell someone you're considering adopting a child, and their stunned face asks the question their mouth refuses to: *Why can't you have your own kids? You can't find a man?*

And then, people question women who might decide to create a birth plan for their children. Those questions include: *How can you just give your baby to someone else? You don't love your baby?*

Wait, what?

Not everyone is bold enough to ask those questions in front of your face, so they gossip about it behind your back instead. Judgement single-handedly prevents many single women from choosing adoption as the gateway to motherhood. They'd rather sacrifice filling the lingering void in their hearts in favor of a little peace and closed mouths. The willing single mother isn't the only one affected by the insensitive fodder, either. Criticism forces birth mothers to raise children they're not sure they can manage. It's not that they don't love their child, but maybe raising them isn't supposed to be part of the plan. It's kind of funny how God's will can be sequestered by social acceptance, only in most cases, not everybody's laughing.

Maybe someone can help me out because I'm a tad confused. See, in the African-American community, we watch, keep, feed, and love each other's children, in unofficial capacities. You know – the village, right? We're play mothers, aunties, god-mommies, and sisters. A plethora of Black women have launched non-profit organizations that provide services to assist children in our communities. Before we feed ourselves, we open our homes and feed the neighborhood. Black women create safe havens to rescue our children from the streets. This is the essence of who we are. So why is the child we're thinking of making part of our forever family not invited to the cookout?

But God.

When the Lord told me He had a child for me and not a man, I thought maybe I needed to go back to the altar. There's no way I could've heard Him correctly. Black folk don't adopt, do they? Once I accepted God's will for me to be a mommy without a man, He placed two people in my life who showed me how to persevere through the peaks and valleys of the adoption process: Mari-Christine Hart-Wright (Chris) and Brian Roberts, who taught me how to embrace the good times and endure the hard ones with grace and class.

Brian Roberts, a public defender and my Divine Nine brother, always wanted to do good for everyone in the entire world. He focused on providing the best love he could for African American males in the foster care system. Not only did he adopt once, but twice welcomed young black men into his home. Brian provided a safety net for at-risk teens, but the impact of his mentorship was often squelched by the fate of their families' circumstances. The outcome wasn't always pretty. Still, Brian maintained his passion for undoing the wrongs inflicted upon young black males. Having witnessed how older children received the short end of the system through his work, he opted to adopt teens. Not only was he non-judgmental of their previous life choices, but he also allowed his walk to be their example.

Then there's my forever sister, Mari-Christine Hart-Wright. She was my sister in Christ, Divine Nine sister, and an amazing social worker. Chris was an empathetic woman who opened her house to everyone but had a soft spot for women needing to get back on their feet. When she encountered a sister whose spirit had been sifted by adversity, Chris extended her arms and said, "Give 'em to me. Do what you need to do, I've got this."

In the twenty years, I knew her, I can't count the number of children Chris gave her heart to; however, when she was asked to officially adopt a family member, she answered the call. And in her first official role as a mother is where I saw Chris persevere through some of the hardest times of her life.

Brian and Chris taught me that devotion gets us through days when we question the amount of love we have to give. Steadfastness covers us when our finances may not look like we want them to, and devotion uplifts us from disappointment when our child wonders why their family doesn't look like many of the ones they see.

May Brian and Chris rest in heaven.

God allowed both of them to plant the adoption seed in my spirit when I wasn't willing to hear it. Coming out on the other side of doubt... their encouragement is a debt I never would be able to repay.

Adoption is the act of giving and promising love. It's persevering through the tough questions and providing even tougher answers. Love is an action verb. Believe me, choosing adoption takes lots of action on your part, but we'll talk more about that later.

Think about how much love a birth mother is filled with to say, "I want to ensure that my baby gets a better shot at life than I can give." That's real power. Feeling a baby growing inside her for nine months, birthing the child, possibly holding the crying newborn, then giving them the blessing of a better life? That takes strength. It's a supreme kind of love. Like the New Testament says, *"The greatest of these is love."* Their sacrifice is Godly love.

Have you noticed how many adoption stories are in the Bible? There's a zillion to choose from, but I'll start with Pharaoh's daughter adopting Moses.

Let's take a journey ... a journey through love, patience, and overall, perseverance through the wait.

"I remain confident of this; I will see the goodness of the Lord in the land of the living. Wait for the Lord; be strong and take heart and wait for the Lord."

Psalm 27:13-14

Chapter 2
The Process

There's an adage that says, "Be careful what you ask God for, you just might get it."

Let's be clear, when we ask for what we want, God will put us to the test to ensure we're ready to manage receiving it. After all, we can't ask for bigger when it's the "little" that buries us. Say we ask God for a larger house, knowing the one we have is a wreck. Not only do we fail to pay the note on time, but the place also looks like a tribute to the television show, *Hoarders*. So, will God trust us with more if the little we have is a mess?

Luke 16:10 tells us, "Whoever can be trusted with very little can also be trusted with much, and whoever is dishonest with very little will also be dishonest with much."

On the other hand, what we want may not be tangible. We pray for God to enlarge our territory and increase the influence of our ministries, singing, preaching, service, and teaching. One thing's for certain and two things for sure: God will put you to the test and ensure you're ready for more. Is your prayer life in order? Do you follow His direction in the ministry, or are you only focused on what you want? There WILL be a test; only God knows what it is and how long you'll endure it.

Despite my weak moments, I grew in my faith. Ecclesiastes 9:11 became prominent in my spiritual life. "The race is not given to the swift."

Race can be interpreted in many ways. In life, the race is considered a marathon or sprint, which are physically and mentally managed differently.

Completing a marathon requires extensive training. Runners must adequately prepare for the twenty-six-mile trek, building strength and confidence through a series of mini-runs. I don't care how cute your leggings are or that the price of the running jacket you found on clearance was slashed in half - endurance is built in increments. Our hearts, lungs, and muscles have to gain strength for the race. Go ahead and try running twenty-six miles without training to build yourself up first. If self-deprecation doesn't get you, the cramps taking over your body will.

Realistically, would you seriously try running long distance without preparing your body for what it's getting into? Knowing I can hop in my car and travel that many miles in fifteen minutes keeps me from putting my body through that physical trauma. That's why mental training is just as important as physical. The small tests along the way alert our minds that it's possible.

God's tests generally involve gradually giving us more to confirm our commitment and ability to take care of what He gives us. The thing is, it's hard for us to consistently cooperate with His will, so He can enlarge our territory. We want the increase, but not always the work that comes with it. God wants us to have better. He wants to give us more. What He doesn't want is to give us what we can't handle. Babies can't chew meat until they grow teeth. Not only do they need teeth, but their organs have to develop to process the food. Our minds must be able to chew the meat God's putting on our plates. Growth takes time.

As much training as marathons require, our bodies need to rest, too. Rest allows our muscles to recover from demanding workouts and prevents mental burnout. Remember, it takes navigating mini sprints before running the big race. God gets us comfortable level by level before He elevates us. Be patient and do the work along the way.

Marathons aren't intended to get you to the finish line quickly; sprints require minimum time commitment. Sure we'll get there faster, but when we're running fast, we're likely to miss beautiful or important details along the way.

Wouldn't it be awful to spend months training, resting your body, and changing your diet, only to fail to make it to the finish line come race day? You don't want your sacrifices to be in vain.

Armed with Ecclesiastes 9:11, I decided it was time to surrender to God's will and not my own. I was intentional about praying and serious about living a life dedicated to God, where I could discern His will versus my own. Was I afraid? Of course! However, being in God's hands is the best place to be. I prayed and pushed worry aside. It was time to build enough to be who God called me to be. I didn't want to waste any more of the time He gave me and was anxious to walk through the doors God would open for me and my family. The anxiety and stress hovering around my heart slowly dissipated, and I was ready.

Through a mountain of prayer, I asked God to grant me patience. What I didn't expect was how He would give it to me. If I could count the number of times I wanted to throw in the towel, I'd only be left with paper towels to dry off with after a bath. But if it weren't for the gift of perseverance, I couldn't imagine where my life would be today.

Chapter 3
The Patience

Single. Black. Female.

Throughout history, unmarried women have been shunned. But should a barren backstory deplete our self-esteem? Of course not – but that doesn't stop it from happening. And when it does, the enemy doesn't waste time writing your story his way.

What's wrong with you?
You work too much.
You travel too much.
Gurl, you'd better take whatever man you can get.
You're too picky.

Most often, the enemy subtly uses those closest to you to convince you that your lack of romance is indeed because of YOU. Then you're left dodging intrusive inquiries and pity-faces when you show up alone at a wedding or family cookout.

Why does society insist that in order to be successful, a woman has to be married? People will have single sisters out here thinking that not having a man cancels the rest of our accomplishments. Don't our degrees mean anything? What about the way we climbed up the career ladder? Can't friendships and family bring just as much happiness?

Fraternizing with negativity makes us give too much attention to what we don't have, rather than focusing on all those things that bring us happiness and joy. We'll put almost everything on hold waiting for a happily ever after that may not even be our destiny.

I'll go to Paris on my honeymoon.
I'll get that house after I get married.
My husband will purchase my mink coat for me.
The car I want is a family car, so I'll wait.

In comparison to biblical times, a woman's role is considered more valuable today. Back then, the birth of a daughter was a loss for the family; girls just didn't have much value. These days, women have more freedom than our biblical counterparts. We don't need permission from our husbands to leave the house. We're able to testify in court and make public appearances by ourselves. And most of all, we have the right to attain roles of position and power. There are notable women in the Bible that we can identify such as Ruth, Esther, and Deborah, who defy the stereotypes of our modern-day social luxuries.

Consider this: During biblical times, women were considered property. Valuable property, but still *property*. There weren't women's marches or a *Me Too* movement to protect us. Essentially, women were considered second-class citizens.

…unfortunately, so are single women today.

You might ask yourself if women are still treated as second-class citizens. Arguably, our world is more sexist than any other word ending in "ist." Although women have shattered glass ceilings over the last few decades, sexism still dominates our existence. Men use women's hormones as the reason they can't rule a nation or a company; however, women have the compassion and empathy necessary to lead. We have the intuition to bridge the gap between business and compassion. And compassion is the vein that keeps life flowing.

When I think about adoption as it relates to the Bible, Pharaoh's daughter is the first woman who comes to mind. As the daughter of a king, her life was lavish, regal and I'm positive she wanted for nothing! I'm assuming men from far and wide were clamoring to marry her, but the Bible doesn't make mention of why she wasn't married. I wonder, did her royal standing protect her from the same humiliation other single women suffer?

I also wonder what the princess's thoughts were when she spotted Moses floating down the River Nile. Immediately recognizing the baby as a Hebrew child, she knew his life was in danger. She knew how adopting him would affect his life, but did she consider how her own would be changed? Knowing her father wouldn't appreciate having that Hebrew child in his home, there's no way the princess didn't have a strong character.

Since Pharaoh had ordered the murder of all Hebrew boys, Moses's mother and his sister, Miriam, put him in the basket to save his life. It took three women to save the boy who as a man, went to Pharaoh demanding, "Let my people go!" before giving us the Ten Commandments and later in his life leading the Israelites to the Promised Land. God appeared to Moses in the form of the burning bush. He's one of two men in the Bible believed to have been taken to Heaven upon his death.

Prior to spotting Moses in the river, the princess was living in the lap of luxury in the palace, doing what she wanted, when she wanted. Did she have any inkling at all how adopting God's Chosen One would change her entire life? God ensured that neither the Nile nor the Pharaoh would kill the man He created to fulfill His ordained purpose. And He used a woman to welcome His Chosen into her heart.

Did the princess who wasn't a bride even want a child? Was Moses the answer to prayers no one knew she prayed? Being an Egyptian woman, surely she'd be crucified for bearing a child out of wedlock; the backlash would've been far worse than a common woman. Maybe she was waiting for a husband and a child. I believe God rewarded her patience by strategically placing baby Moses in her path as she bathed.

Much like Pharaoh's daughter was rewarded for her perseverance, God rewarded my resilience while waiting to adopt. In 2004, I completed my first adoption certification; however, the call I received that a baby boy had just been born in DC didn't come until 2011. Seven years is a long time to expect a call, especially when you anticipate it taking no longer than a year. But when the call finally came, I couldn't contain my excitement!

I didn't waste any time purchasing furniture, wall hangings, and other cute items that caught my eye. I made a list of baby names, godparents, and any unique clothing items that might not be available in the next year. It's a good thing only a few people knew I'd begun the process or I'm sure they would've constantly hassled me about the status.

It wasn't long before hurdles were added to the marathon I was running. The social workers probed into my background so much, they ended up knowing more about my life than my parents. An extensive home study was used to determine whether my life, history, and home could provide an emotional, physical, and financially stable environment for my child. *My child*. Praise God I committed to the endeavor before I realized how daunting the entire thing would be. Poking around in the prospective parents' pasts takes time; researching birth, marriage and criminal records sometimes takes more time than we have patience. So while I was being subjected to a rigorous look into my past and present, my baby was floating down the Nile, waiting to be adopted.

Never one to be deterred, I ran from municipal center to municipal center, clearing hurdles as I gathered documents and checked them off my overwhelming *to-do* list. I have to admit, visiting police headquarters to obtain my background clearance wasn't a trip that I looked forward to. Not that I had anything to hide, I just didn't know what to expect. The only experience I had with police stations was what I'd seen on television. I saved that trip for last.

As a finance professional, I figured the monetary requirements would be my sweet spot, but the actual requirements quickly turned it sour. See, the IRS is very aware of our economic standing and cares about the money we earn. Not how we spend it, but that they get their share of what we bring in. The adoption agency; however, wanted a balance sheet of everything coming in and going out. They literally gauge our parental competency by what we spend versus what we earn. Most importantly, social workers are concerned with whether or not we have money saved in case of emergencies. It's crucial they know that you can provide, not only emotionally, but financially for the child.

…which leads us back to Pharaoh's daughter.

Pharaoh's daughter didn't let the fact that she wasn't married deter her from rescuing baby Moses from the Nile. God filled her heart with compassion, and she adopted His Chosen One, who lived with her in the palace of the King of Egypt. What if she saw the baby, and decided to let him go? How much different would their lives have been?

On my journey to motherhood, I showered many children with love and compassion while I waited. I almost have more godchildren than I can count, whom I traveled, shopped, and ate with, and enjoyed sleepovers. If nothing else, I was enjoying my practice run as a mommy. I even took one of my goddaughters and godsons (who are cousins), on a road trip to Virginia Beach, Virginia. The sun provided the backdrop for an awesome beach weekend, and the roads weren't congested as we eased down the highway with very few stops. To this day, whenever I hear a particular song on the radio, memories of sand, seafood, and that special time bonding with my babies, fill my thoughts.

Pharaoh's daughter was strong. A weak woman couldn't defy the King by adopting the very child he intended to kill and bring him to live in the palace. God gave her the strength she needed to confront her father and love baby Moses.

Through the seven years I waited for God to bless me and my family with a little bundle of joy, resiliency and strength guided me. However, perseverance helped me be patient when the adoption agency informed me that most birth mothers prefer to place their children with married couples. I was crushed, but I wasn't defeated. I knew what God said, and I refused to accept anything less than His promise.

Pharaoh's daughter was simply at the river with her handmaids, taking a bath. I often remind myself about that part - she wasn't there alone; she had her village with her. I'm sure they encouraged and helped her to pull baby Moses from the water. Remember, the village isn't just for the child, the village is also in place for the parent.

To keep my forever family hopes alive, I surrounded myself with single women who were also adopting children. Being around those ladies encouraged me that someday, adoption would happen for me.

Initially, we helped each other complete our forms, enjoyed dinner together, and cheered each other on as placements were finalized. This group was important for me because the first step of the home study was to successfully complete parenting courses. I was the only single black female in my group. The couples were nice, but honestly, being alone was awkward and uncomfortable.

Now I knew the adoption agency didn't mean any harm, but the questions they asked during group were tailored to couples. One question

I remember vividly is, *how would you handle custody in the event of a divorce*? I loved it because since I wasn't married, I didn't even have to consider divorce.

Until I did.

I hadn't given much thought to the fact that many men prefer not to date single mothers. I brushed it off under the guise that God would bring a man into my life who would love both me and my child, unconditionally. To me, being a mother through adoption would save them the aggravation of *baby daddy* drama, right?

My new group of sisters helped me see the importance of aligning yourself with a group of people who look like you, share similar ideas, and strive to accomplish the same goals as you, not just in adoption, but in every aspect of life. I don't know how I could've navigated such a major life change without them.

One thing I asked myself while completing this chapter was how I persevered as I saw other women receiving their babies? Did not having anyone ask her father for her hand in marriage and being a single mother make Pharaoh's daughter feel like an outcast? I'm sure it must have. And in the twentieth and twenty-first centuries, the same pain is still prevalent. I won't even lie - if you're asked to be someone's wife knowing you'll end up divorced because it's not a fit, you have to say no to the dress and the ring. But doing what's best for you ends up getting you ostracized, because obviously, it's not the man, it's you. Sigh…

Prayer helped me persevere through my situation. This was also a time when I learned and grew spiritually as my discernment was sharpened. While I still didn't have the husband or child I was believing God for, I spent time learning to accurately hear His voice. We can want something so bad, that we mistake our voice for God's; I needed to learn the difference if I was going to make it.

The best way I can describe God's voice is to ask yourself does what you hear line up with His Word. If the nudging pushes you out of your comfort zone, it's very likely God is trying to tell you something. If it doesn't line up with what His Word says, it's probably not Him you're hearing. For example, some people convince themselves God told them someone else's husband or wife is theirs. Nope. No ma'am. No, sir - adultery doesn't line up with His Word. Remember, God is all about the marathon, not the sprint. He will encourage you to grow before He elevates you. Coveting doesn't reflect growth, it's an indicator of immaturity in the Word.

Learning to understand God's Word and His will is another way I persevered while waiting. My desire to get closer to Him grew so intense, I studied and earned a Certificate in Biblical Studies through a local church. The funny thing was, I thought I'd just take a few introductory courses to help with my inspirational writing, but my instructors were so knowledgeable about the things of God, I ended up delving deeper and deeper so I could know more about Him, too. It wasn't easy, but it was worth it as God built my patience muscle. Although I was in a holding pattern, He knew what I needed to help me be the parent He wanted me to be. In His timing.

Instead of driving myself crazy while I waited, I used my time to be productive and do the things I loved, like traveling and visiting places I wanted to experience. With my mother as my travel partner, we trekked to Europe during a ten-day excursion. This trip along with others showed me the value of traveling with a parent. My mother and I had the opportunity to chat about things that would've been difficult to discuss at home. With our guards down and vulnerabilities exposed, our transparency brought us closer. Based upon this trip, I vowed to travel with my child and create these same types of memories, and bond. In the meantime, I waited. And after two years, the call came in. The one I sacrificed my time, effort, and heart to answer. My life would be forever changed. This was the placement call.

Or so I thought.

An unusually warm, sunny spring day found me sitting at my desk. I was using a folded piece of paper to fan with when my office phone rang; it was my social worker. I was hopeful that after so long, maybe she wasn't calling to remind me that, yet another form needed updating as per her usual calls. As bad as I wanted the news on the other end of that phone to be exactly what I wanted to hear, I didn't get too excited as I answered. I wasn't ready to hear that what I prayed and waited for was finally manifesting. Good thing I was already sitting down.

I don't know if it was good news or a hot flash, but I fanned harder as the words my social worker said slowly penetrated my ears: After pouring over a plethora of prospective parents, a teen mother chose me to raise her baby girl. In the back of my mind, I'd always believed being single wouldn't be a deal-breaker, even though that's how many of our stories have ended. As much as I feared rejection, deep within I knew *someone* would embrace me in spite of what was considered less than ideal circumstances.

After hearing there was a mother who was actually interested in me, the rest of the conversation was a blur. All I heard was there was a baby on the way. At the end of the call, she advised me she'd call me back in a day or two with specifics, including arranging a meeting with the mother. I was so excited to meet the woman whom I'd be connected to through this open adoption. Why had I opted for an open one? Because if I were the birth mother, I couldn't imagine not having any contact with my child for the rest of my life. I was looking forward to this meeting; it was finally my time.

Two days later, my phone rang. Unlike last time, I was ecstatic to answer and find out when I'd be meeting my child's mother. I was almost woozy with excitement, until the social worker's distressed voice deflated my upbeat attitude. Almost tearfully, she apologized profusely, telling me the teen's mother encouraged her to go with a couple as opposed to me.

My heart sank. I'm not sure how long I cried, but the tears fell until I was completely drained. My days were filled with what could've been, imagining what life with my daughter would have been like. Would she be a girly-girl who loved dolls and playing in tiaras? Or would she love sports and be the one to change her generation?

Wrapped in full-blown grief over a child who wasn't even born, I sank deep into depression. As the days slowly drug by, I suffered from insomnia and climbed into a funk for at least a month. Was God testing me? Was this a cruel joke the universe was playing on me? This entire time, I'd been diligently listening to God - what lesson was I supposed to learn? Eventually, I chalked up my misfortune to building those muscles of patience, picked myself up, and moved on. But I'll never forget that experience.

After the adoption fell through, two more years passed. More paperwork. More interviews. More attempts by the enemy to frustrate me. Not much had changed on my end – especially the waiting. One time, a new social worker called me, and I responded to her with short, terse, one-word responses. S*he's never going to recommend you to a birth parent if you keep acting like this,* I thought. Realizing I was sabotaging myself, I quickly got myself together. If God was testing me, I was determined to pass.

My friend, Chris, encouraged me to get my paperwork updated. She never let me talk about quitting. It was a good thing too, because a short while later, I was contacted by a sister adoption agency in Las Vegas who matched me with a birth mother. This placement would require me to live in Vegas for at least thirty days to establish residency. I pushed the past heartbreak from my mind and searched for an extended stay residence. God had brought me that far...I was willing to take the extra steps to meet Him at my purpose. He blessed me with the gift of discernment, the ability to recognize His voice, and His will as I persevered. It was on!

Once I secured housing, all I needed was the date from the agency to arrive so the clock would start ticking on my out-of-state residency. Not only did I have to prepare to live out of state alone for a month with a brand-new baby, but I also had to purchase what my baby would need back home upon our return. Bottles, pampers, a crib, clothes. I needed *everything*. I considered having a baby shower for a quick minute, but decided it was best to wait until I got back home.

So there I was at my desk again, preparing for an afternoon meeting when the phone rang. Again, I recognized the number and my heart almost jumped out of my chest. It was the social worker. I took a deep breath and answered.

This time, I was advised that everything was in order, but the birth mother asked if I could pay her money. Honestly, I can't remember what the extra money was for. Taken aback, I thought about it for a second before agreeing to do it. Please understand, adoptions are not free. I'd already paid the agency's fees, but I was so anxious for this to be over and begin life with my child that I was willing to pay the extra money directly to the birth mother.

After scrambling to put money into a secondary account, I waited to hear more. A few days later, I received another call: The birth mother needed money for rent. Ummm...at this point, it felt like a shake-down. Before I could say what I thought about paying even more money out, God told me this wasn't the baby boy He intended for me to adopt.

Please Lord, not again.

My level of patience instantly went from toddler to teen in a matter of minutes. If this was a matter of building muscle, I probably could've bench-pressed at least three hundred pounds at this point. When I heard myself say *I'll wait*, I knew in my spirit this baby wasn't the one God had chosen for me. Had I gone to Vegas and jumped through all the hoops the birth mother demanded, there was going to be more. A lot more. My attitude changed, and I didn't trust her anymore. Where there's no trust…there's no God. I canceled my trip to Vegas and stopped the adoption.

For the record, I didn't ask God to give me the patience of Job, but every time a placement fell through, I thought maybe that's what He was trying to give me. As much as I wanted to give up, I wanted to stay in the race even more. I hadn't come this far to quit. I was somewhat broken; however, my competitive spirit insisted I stay in the marathon.

Sometimes, the hardest part of a journey is keeping your patience until the end. How do you know how close you are to your goal? In an actual marathon, there are markers and people rooting you toward the finish line. In adoption, you never know when a birth mother or father will pick yours from the mounds of applications they review.

There were four years between my first application to become an adoptive parent until now. I had a feeling I'd endure more heartache before I crossed the finish line.

Chapter 4
The Options

Baby or marriage? Was it a choice? Presumably so.

When I turned forty-three, a friend introduced me to a nice man who was ten years older than me. Although marriage wasn't a priority for me, I hadn't ruled it out, either. I was open to dating, and if that led to a committed relationship, I'd be happy with that. The thing was, I wanted to be sure anyone I thought of becoming serious with knew about my intentions to adopt and accepted me as well as my child. In spite of past disappointments, that was a deal-breaker I wasn't willing to relinquish. As I casually got to know potential suitors, I decided not to broach the subject of adoption until I felt a strong connection with someone, and the feeling was mutual.

My friend introduced me to a gentleman who checked all my boxes: confident, kind, funny, and spiritually, we were on the same level. He was retired from the armed services and worked a full-time job he seemed to enjoy. He was the ultimate gentleman, not to mention I easily fell for a well-dressed man in a suit, which my new friend wore well. I don't believe I ever touched a doorknob or handle when I was out with him. He knew how to treat a lady, and started falling for me, hard. I liked him, but unfortunately not as much as he liked me.

After we'd dated less than six months, he surprised me with a pair of stunning pearl earrings. Although my love language is *acts of service,* this gift took my breath away. One evening, he planned a romantic dinner at an expensive restaurant. The setting was everything I wanted for an evening out with my man; too bad I only liked him as a friend. I wasn't even physically attracted to him, but I thought I'd at least try to see where things went with us.

I've always heard that relationships work best when a man loves a woman more than she loves him. I can unequivocally confirm...that is not the truth. At least he never made me feel uncomfortable. In an effort to ensure I wasn't taking advantage of him, at the end of our dates, I snatched the bill from the table to keep him from paying it. "Only this time," he said with a sigh.

This night, as we savored our meal over a nice glass of cabernet, I slipped in the question.

"How do you feel about children?"

I swear to this day, that man almost choked on a forkful of his medium-well ribeye.

"I'm a man of a certain age," he stammered, "I can't imagine a baby in my life at this time. I want to settle down and travel with my wife."

Crickets.

If he'd responded differently, would I have grown to like him in a different way? Could I have fallen in love with him? I didn't stick around long enough to find out; we lost touch. No, I didn't ghost him, though. I simply explained how adoption was in the cards for me, and that it was an important part of my life. Needless to say, we went our separate ways.

Faith played a large role in my ability to let go. Of course, I thought about how married life without a child could be, flying to exotic, romantic locales, without a worry in the world. If nothing else throughout this thing, I learned that the enemy was trying to make me feel as though my desire to raise a child on my own was crazy, and I ended up questioning myself.

Was I doing things backward?
Does God want me to desire marriage?

I banished those thoughts from my mind and hid in God's Word as I continued traveling and loving on the little ones who were already in my life. Isn't it funny how we can be minding our business and boom, something – or someone else we think we want drops into our lives? That's exactly what happened when I unexpectedly met another man who I actually liked and was instantly attracted to. He was funny and sensitive, but…emotionally unavailable. He strung me along as though we could become a couple. Dude went as far as to establish a committed relationship with me. Turns out, the commitment was one-sided.

It was the summer of 2011, and we went to several concerts together. He also attended my Biblical Studies Certificate graduation. He had two children and didn't see a problem with my unconventional journey toward motherhood.

Or so I thought.

Keep in mind that all this time, I'd only had two social workers. The first one lasted five years, but as she made plans to retire, she transferred me to one of her coworkers so we could establish a relationship and get to know one another. Thank God I stayed on my original social worker's mind. That July, she called and told me that a birth mother contacted her from the hospital, asking to process her adoption. She immediately thought of me.

The number three is special to me, not only because it's said to be a charm, but because I was third on a line of five when I was initiated into Delta Sigma Theta Sorority, Inc. That held my head high and gave me the optimism I needed to follow through a third round of processing. But I knew my child would be worth it.

I shared the news with the new guy in my life, who sounded just as excited as I was to have another chance, yet over the course of the next few weeks, as I prepared for the baby's homecoming, he slowly pulled away. His calls were less and wrote exactly what I needed to see on the wall – my 'Baby Moses' had come between us, but there's no worry or failure when God intervenes.

Be careful of who you share information with.

Marriage or baby?

Would the stars ever align for me?

Was I asking for too much?

With these questions gnawing at my spirit, Psalm 37:4 reverberated through my mind.

"Delight yourself in the Lord and He will give you the desires of your heart."

I committed myself to knowing God better, establishing a relationship. I was willing to wait on Him because God knew what I needed better than I did.

Psalm 37:7 goes on to instruct us to *"Be still before the Lord and wait patiently for Him."*

I knew what I wanted, and I knew what God wanted for me. He wouldn't have brought me that far to abandon me.

My perseverance muscle grew stronger, and I was ready to flex it.

Chapter 5
Answering the Call

SEVEN WHOLE DAYS.

I couldn't get Toni Braxton's song from my head when Ms. Smith told me that I'd need to give her a response within a week.

After everything I'd gone through with previous placements, you'd think that I wouldn't need more than seven seconds to say yes.

Not so.

For reasons unbeknownst to me, fear reared its ugly head and stalled me. My parents and other immediate family supported everything I'd ever thought about doing, so I knew they'd be there for me, but I also knew those late-night cries of hunger or wet pampers would fall solely on me. As visions of funds flying out of my bank account inundated my thoughts, fear wrapped itself around me like an anaconda, attempting to squeeze the faith out of me. It was awful. Adoption agencies don't typically reach out to potential adoptive parents over the age of forty-five; at forty-seven, my shelf life was dwindling.

To buy time, I asked if I could meet the little fella. With my family tagging along in another car, we drove to the agency and met the baby's foster parents, social worker, and the beautiful baby boy himself.

Let's be honest here, the average gestation time to get used to the idea of bringing a baby home is nine months. I had a week. Let's not even talk about purchasing items and setting up his room.

I know what you're thinking.

Didn't you have the room set up?

Somewhat.

Didn't you have a ton of money just sitting in a bank account ready for the call?

Nope.

What's funny about all of this? To get ready for my child, I'd moved to a larger home. Which meant more money. I prepared for this alright… before it was within my grasp. That's the difference between *before* the call and *after* the call.

On the day of the visit, I worked a half-day without finishing any of my tasks. Blame it on my lack of focus. To relieve my rebelling stomach, I rummaged through my purse and found some aspirin. I popped one in my mouth to calm my nerves and ward off a headache. During lunch hour, I picked up Mom and Dad and headed for the adoption agency. We rode in silence, keeping our excitement in check. When we arrived, my sister, brother-in-law, and baby nephew were waiting in the parking lot for us. As we waited for the foster parents to arrive, we joked about how long it took us to get to this point.

I heard him before I saw him. His cries of hunger echoed through the foyer the moment they entered the building. His foster mother abruptly walked into the office, placed a chunky baby boy with beautiful fat cheeks in my lap, and handed me a bottle. As I fed him, I adjusted the adorable baby blue overall short set he wore.

It felt surreal. I couldn't believe we were in this place, both literally and figuratively. I was bonding with my son over a bottle of milk. When a woman is pregnant, the physical connection during the gestation period offers many opportunities to connect. Many mothers sing, read and dance with their babies. Dancing releases endorphins. When the mother feels good, so does the baby. Even the act of rubbing her belly while talking introduces the baby to her voice, prompting the little one to kick in response.

Bonding in any relationship is important. Although unconventional, this was my first opportunity to create *our* moment. I hummed and sang while he gulped his milk. It was hard to take my eyes off his beautiful face. Once the bottle was empty, I placed a cloth on my blouse and laid his head on my shoulder. It didn't even take a minute before the biggest belch erupted from his throat, directly into my ear. Everyone in the room laughed, including me. Bonding over burping. This was easy. It was natural. It was good.

My entire family snapped pictures with the baby. He sat on my mother's lap with my father in the chair next to her, leaning in with the broadest smile. My sister and brother-in-law - the proud auntie and uncle, jumped in the next picture. Last but not least, we took pictures of the baby and his soon-to-be cousin, my eight-month-old nephew. Looking at those pictures now, it's amazing to see how our smiles not only exude from our mouths but pours through the light in our eyes. My sister captured moments as I stroked baby boy's bushy eyebrows and admired his full eyelashes. As a grown woman, I craved for lashes that long.

Before we knew it, the hour with our little one was nearing an end. As we said our goodbyes, he sneezed, and a huge glob of phlegm escaped his nose. Nothing like cleaning a baby's nose to create more bonding. In the past, I may have been taken aback, but when baby boy did it, I deemed it special.

We said our goodbyes to the social worker and the foster parents who were gracious to my entire family. It takes a special heart to care for a child, knowing it's only for a short period of time. We spoke privately for a few minutes and his foster mother shared baby boy's sleeping and eating habits.

We left, and I went back to *living single*: sleeping in, going to bed late, and hanging out on weekends. What - you didn't think this would end with me strapping the baby in a car seat and beginning our happily ever after, did you?

Remember, this was the summer of 2011 in Washington, DC. The men of Omega Psi Phi Fraternity, Inc. held their bi-annual conclave in the city. There are perks to living in a major metropolitan area, like large organizations hosting their annual meetings and celebrations there.

After getting my hair and nails done for these particular festivities, all that was left to do was pick a slamming outfit to set off my new 'do. Knowing I was the bomb, I used the mirror to style and profile in my white, asymmetrical, knee-length, half-shoulder *freakum* dress.

Don't judge me, good people.

My friends and I bounced from our cars and rolled up at the party. Brothers we hadn't seen in years were there, and we had a wonderful time catching up. Although the ladies and I enjoyed the music and had a blast running into people from our college days, there was one thing that made me sad...we were alone. And we'd go home alone. Once the party was over, we'd stroll up to our driveways, slip the key in the front door, and walk into an empty house. Then we'd go to sleep with no one else there.

Going home to my lonely reality that night, I knew what I wanted most in life: a family. That beautiful baby boy I'd met, fed, held, kissed, and let burp in my face was my family. I was positive. Nothing could shake the image of those juicy cheeks from my mind. He was my son.

With all doubt gone, I flew into action, starting with calling my social worker to request another meeting with the foster parents, and the opportunity to bond with the baby more.

She granted my request.

This time when we met, I knew what to expect and was more confident. The humidity was thick as sludge, which is typical for July in my city. This time, I made the trip alone. As I pulled into the parking lot, my family stood next to their cars as my sister pointed to an open space for me to park. The sleeveless dress I wore flowed behind me as I jumped out of the car and we rushed through the door.

We were ushered into the same meeting room where we met before and within minutes, baby boy was in my lap again. I admired his little one-piece denim short set as he grinned at me with those big, luscious lashes fluttering. This time we played. I kissed his fat little cheeks and noticed he was still nursing a runny nose. His foster mother explained that he never really got over it, maybe because he may have had allergies. Compassion stirred inside me for that bundle of joy. When I wiped and cleaned his nose, I knew he was my baby.

This was when I felt the desire to kneel down and pick my baby up out of the River Nile.

I hate to sound cliché, but I received an epiphany. Not only did I hear God's voice, but I felt His spirit. Before I left, I informed my social worker that I wanted to proceed with my forever family. That day, I knew I'd finally get to the last stage of the placement. Weight lifted from me; I knew it was God because the fear was gone. This was my turning point. Warmth, compassion, and love filled my heart.

I often think about what would have happened if I pressed my will during the previous potential placements.

Would I have felt that warmth?

Would the cloud of fear have left my spirit?

I knew the answer to those questions. God doesn't dwell in doubt or fear.

Unlike Pharaoh's daughter who knew she wouldn't find favor with her father for pulling baby Moses from the Nile, the patriarch of my family couldn't wait for us to bring our little baby home. Dad sat in the office observing our interactions, then leaned forward in his seat, stroked the child's hair, and asked, "You gonna do it, right?"

My father's question gave me wings.

I knew at that moment that persevering through the wait and allowing God to build my patience muscle was so that I could learn to know when a gift was from Him. I'd feel comfortable saying, 'no, this is not in His will'.

Weeping may endure for a moment, but joy comes in the morning.

I almost shouted right there in the social worker's office. My days of weeping were over, it was finally *morning*. I was a mother in need of a son. Baby boy needed a mother.

I was almost at the end of the marathon.

Almost.

Chapter 6
The Village

Have you ever noticed how the same woman who sent baby Moses floating down the Nile in the basket was also present when Pharaoh's daughter rescued him? Miriam, Moses's sister, immediately intervened as the princess pulled the baby from the water, asking if she wanted her to fetch a Hebrew woman to nurse the child. Once she received an affirmative response, Miriam quickly ran off to get Moses's birth mother. I'm not sure how long Moses was in the basket, but I imagine he cried his little lungs out from hunger pangs. They didn't have Similac back then. Someone had to feed the baby.

This is the power of *the village*.

Before we left the office after our second visit, my social worker handed me a few forms needing updating, which wasn't a problem because I knew where to get everything I needed to fill them out. This should be easy since it seemed like I'd done it at least one hundred times before. The foster family and I exchanged contact information so she could fill me in on baby boy's schedule, habits, and overall health.

The power of the village.

My village and I scrambled to round up nursery items and other things for baby boy. People donated barely used dressers, my close friends gifted a crib and bedding items. We tore down the aisles of Target and Walmart, purchasing clothes, bottles, and burping cloths. I scooped up as much as I could, but of course, my friends regulated me to only a few items. Blame it on the baby shower they were planning. I love them.

Although Moses' birth mother and Miriam sent the baby down the Nile to save his life, they stayed vested in his life and continued caring for him. This little baby had people doing everything they could to help him successfully transition from one family to another. This is another reason why Moses' birth story and subsequent adoption resonated with me. Baby boy had people who literally embraced him from the time he was birthed. His foster family fed him, loved on him, and learned to detect and understand his needs, desires, and schedules. And hopefully, soon, they'd pass on their knowledge to me, and I'd learn the same.

After seven years of enduring the process, seven days was a short time to say, "Yes, I'm ready." But when I agreed to this blessing from God, I needed to exercise my patience muscle while I waited for those last few documents to be certified. It was hard but necessary. I needed to show God I had faith in His plan for my forever family.

Following a short wait, we received *the call* confirming that the third time was indeed, the charm for me.

My next time seeing baby boy in the social worker's office wouldn't be a visit; it was our homecoming day.

Before we picked him up to take him to his new home, I felt like a mother. It was as if my water broke, and I was headed to the hospital to give birth. I imagined that I'd think of everything as if it were my last time living single.

It's my last time waking up at home alone.

It's my last time jumping into the shower without a baby monitor.

It's my last time running out of the house without thinking about breakfast.

Instead, I thought of everything as if it were my first day as a mother.

This is my first time hearing the birds singing outside my window as a mother.

This is my first time getting dressed as a mother.

This is my first time leaving this house as a mother.

My typical mornings consisted of placing my feet on the floor, jumping into the shower, getting dressed, and leaving the house without giving much thought to my routine. All that instantly changed, though. The world was brand new. It was odd; an out-of-body experience that I loved every minute of. In life, there are some big days that stay etched in your mind. This day ranked as one of the most important in my life.

"For I know the plans I have for you," declares the Lord, *"plans to prosper you and not to harm you, plans to give you hope and a future."*

I knew God was in control of my life and had good things in store for me and my son. I prayed the Lord would be right by our side in the valley. He gave me goals and purpose before His plans manifested in my life. See, people are three-dimensional. We have multiple desires, and one doesn't have to outweigh the others. But God held onto my hand the entire time I journeyed to my son.

Psalm 27:13-14, are very popular passages of scripture. *"I remain confident of this; I will see the goodness of the Lord in the land of the living. Wait for the Lord; be strong and take heart and wait for the Lord."*

These two promises of God spoke to me. As I clung to those scriptures, they warmed my spirit like a crackling fire on a cold winter's night.

I was *confident* that I was this precious little boy's mother. I knew everything I'd *hoped* for would be everything I imagined and more. God soothed my anxious spirit as I moved on to the next phase: Naming my child.

I always thought I'd adopt a baby girl. Thoughts of bows, barrettes, and cute little dresses danced in my head. I'd even selected a girl's name. Since my faith was important to me, that's the name I wanted for my daughter - Faith.

As for me and my house ...

Another popular verse of scripture comes from Joshua 24:15. Joshua was Moses' second in command and his God-chosen successor. Following the death of Moses, Joshua led the new generation of Israelites into the Promised Land after wandering in the wilderness for forty years. Joshua trusted that God would give them the land He'd promised. His faith in God's promises is a character trait that I wanted instilled in my son.

As an African American male in America, there comes a time when you're going to have to fight. Not necessarily with the intention of hurting someone, but daily we fight insecurities such as doubt and fear. We struggle with anger, anxiety, depression, and other emotions that attempt to rob us of the joy God intended for us.

There are two angels named in the Bible. Gabriel, who appeared before the Virgin Mary, announcing that God had chosen her to give birth to His son, Jesus. Archangel Michael is the warrior angel, who engages in spiritual combat. He's depicted as contending, fighting, or standing against evil principalities. In a child's life, standing against evil principalities could mean standing up to peer pressure, or defending themselves against a bully or an aggressive classmate. I prayed that my son would have the spirit of John Lewis, recognizing that *Good Trouble* is sometimes necessary.

Although Michael the Archangel is powerful, he's totally committed to the Lord's will. His submission to God doesn't take away his power or authority. Michael knows who he is in the Lord and his purpose. He's totally content and satisfied with the role that the Lord has assigned him. That's a life lesson. Being content with the gifts, attributes, and purposes that God instills in us is important to achieving overall happiness and fulfillment.

Because both names resonated with me, I prayed that my son would personify the qualities that the names *Joshua* and *Michael* represent.

Good things come to those who wait.

October 6, 2011, proved to me that *great* things come to those who not only waited but did so with obedience and faithfulness. There's a certain amount of humility that comes along with practicing patience. On a day-to-day basis, we don't know how things will work out, but remembering God's Word says *all things work for your good* became my constant prayer. Maurette Brown Clarke's *It Ain't Over* was the song that carried me through. My posture was gratefulness for everything I had in my life.

I'd prepared my home, my heart, and selected names. The day had finally come to bring my little baby home. A few days earlier, the department of motor vehicles fit the car seat safely in the back. Although I drove to the social services agency alone, I didn't leave alone. I anticipated officially getting my baby in my arms as his mother would take a few hours, but it didn't.

After signing a few more papers, I spoke to the foster family a short while. My heart went out to the foster mother and father. I couldn't imagine loving and caring for a child for months, then giving him or her to their forever parents, but that's a part of knowing God's plan for our lives. That glorious foster family allowed God to use them to stand in the gap for little ones until their new parents carried them home. It's God's work.

What touched my heart the most that day was that the foster father couldn't let go. The mother gave me pictures of the baby with their family, along with one of the shirts she wore so just in case the little fella missed her, I'd have something with her scent. She reconciled to saying goodbye, but her husband found it hard to release him. In a touching move, she leaned over and whispered to her husband, "It's time."

Then he placed the baby in my arms.

We agreed to send pictures and cards, a promise that we've kept and will continue. After all, I'd gone through to get to this point – the part where the dream comes true, I silently vowed to offer any comfort that I could. My heart was connected to their bittersweet goodbye. Every year, we mail them Easter and Christmas cards and are overjoyed to receive theirs in return.

It takes a village.

As we strapped Joshua Michael Johnson into his car seat, I smiled from ear to ear. My entire family ushered me out of the social services agency for the last time, this time, joined by baby boy. My son. Everyone cooed and kissed Joshua's cheeks before I strapped him in the car.

In a recent episode of *This Is Us*, we got a glimpse into each family's experience when they brought their children home from the hospital. It reminded me of my first ride home with Joshua Michael, which was both exciting and nerve wrecking at the same time. Although I drove alone to the agency, my sister chauffeured us back to my house so I could sit in the back with Joshua. My eyes stayed glued on him as we traveled through the city over bumps that hit harder than they did on the ride to pick him up. With wide eyes, he watched as I adjusted the soft blanket over his legs and waist.

"How long will it take for him to cry?" I asked myself, but he stayed awake and didn't whimper or whine.

People often take babies on car rides to get them to sleep, but when we pulled up to my assigned parking space, Joshua was wide awake, curiosity oozing from his eyes. The sandman wasn't coming any time soon.

"Don't worry about taking anything in. I'll get the stuff later," my sister said as she scurried to the rear of the SUV to assist us. "Let's just get him in the house."

After agreeing, I gingerly removed the seat from its base. "Lil' baby, we're home."

I turned Joshua's carrier toward the trees, highlighted with yellow, orange, and crimson. The climb up the twelve steps to enter my condo wasn't as bad as I thought it would be. After crossing the threshold, I marched to the couch. This was the moment I'd been waiting for. Removing Joshua from the seat and rocking him was a moment I'd never forget. And since my sister - our personal paparazzi, was there, I have a wonderful picture that captured our day. Peace and comfort exude from the image. I still feel the love. A love Supreme.

"Wait for the Lord; be strong and take heart and wait for the Lord."

Psalms 27:14.

surprise us, which was fine with me. I was advised of the date, and that's all I knew. So, in the meantime, I warned everyone to wear comfortable shoes, because we were going to be doing a lot of line dancing, specifically the Wobble. I was ready to party!

Even though I was already aware of what was going down, I was still startled by a resounding "Surprise!" as I entered through the building's double doors. Since Joshua had just come home, I briefly allowed everyone a short time to admire him before sending him with a babysitter during the festivities.

It was close to the beginning of football season and the hostesses dressed alike, clad as referees, my crew produced an event that everyone enjoyed. The games were fun and didn't interfere with mingling time. The food was scrumptious and catered to every pallet from vegetarian to soul food. Whatever anyone's taste buds desired, the village made sure it was there.

We were jamming hard when one of the hostesses called out, "Gift time," to the crowd. They were so comical because if a guest didn't follow directions, they'd throw flags indicating penalties on the field. Needless to say, when it was time to gather around to open the presents, our guests knew it was best to adhere to directions.

One quirky aspect of most showers is the crazy hat that's made for the guest of honor.

"Don't throw away any bows, ribbons, or other embellishments that'll make this hat the best ever," a hostess announced, eyeballing the boxes and gift bags. Joshua and I were truly blessed with amazing gifts and an outpouring of love. One gift, in particular, spoke to the essence of Psalms 27:14. *"Wait for the Lord; be strong and take heart and wait for the Lord."*

While on a girls' trip to St. John in the Virgin Islands, one of my best friends purchased a plate set. She knew the plan was to adopt a baby girl

Chapter 7
The Next Episode

A light afternoon wind greeted Joshua and I as we left home to meet family and friends for our baby shower. For me, the celebration was a milestone marking the ending of disappointment, ushering in joy and renewed hope. We were showered with gifts, plenty of advice, and most of all, love. One of the best loves of all.

I couldn't fight the excitement and as tears of joy eased down my cheeks. I'd become adept at getting the baby in and out of the car and couldn't wait to walk into the community room to the smell of fried chicken and the sight of Mom's baked beans everyone loved so much. My aunts, uncles, godparents, and other members of our village were ready to meet Joshua Michael Johnson, and he was ready for them. Due to the uncertainty of Joshua's homecoming day, the village couldn't and the design was perfect. She kept it in its original packaging until the adoption was complete. When God answered my prayers and blessed me with Joshua, she still wanted to give me the gift. When she opened the packaging to wrap it for the shower, the receipt fell from the bag. She shared the date with everyone at the shower, which revealed the biggest miracle of all: the wait had been seven whole years.

"The gift that God gave Terri was the obedience, patience, and unwavering faith that He would give her the desire of her heart. While Joshua is truly a live and in-person gift, Terri's ability to stay faithful was a true gift from God," Rhonda eloquently spoke to each heart in the room. God was in the midst of the shower. But where else would He be? He'd stayed with me during the entire process. That's why I could never stop running the marathon.

"...a crown of beauty instead of ashes..."
Isaiah 61:3

Chapter 8
The Greatest Adoption Story

The Bible depicts how God put various people in Moses's life to help him become the man who would lead the Israelites to the Promised Land. Having studied the intricate part Pharaoh's daughter played in his destiny through adoption, now let's review the ultimate adoption story of the ages: Jesus Christ and Joseph, His earthly father.

During Christmas, we often think of the Virgin Mary giving birth to Jesus Christ, almost neglecting to reflect on Joseph's story and how God choosing him to raise Jesus was just as important as Jesus's birth mother.

Can you imagine telling the man that you're engaged to that you're pregnant with a baby who isn't his? Then your fiancée trying to justify the situation by trying to convince you an angel appeared to her, saying God is the baby's father? What would you do?

Let's look at this from the man's perspective.

I'd believe either I was being lied to, or she lost her mind. I mean, come on – an angel? Immaculate Conception? Really? Either my woman is lying or off. Either way, I'm not buying what she's selling. Like Joseph, I would leave, but at least he did it in a way that wouldn't embarrass Mary. Joseph intended to end their relationship quietly and maintain Mary's integrity as he broke off the relationship.

That's when God stepped in.

He sent an angel to Joseph affirming Mary's message about the child she was carrying being conceived by the Holy Spirit.

As a man of faith, integrity, and obedience, Joseph married Mary.

So what are the similarities between Joseph and Jesus's adoption story and mine?

God ordained both of our adoptions. They weren't a secondary option or a Plan B. Although four hundred years had passed, Jesus fulfilled Old Testament prophesy that the Messiah would be a direct descendent of King David. Faithful Jews were still waiting on the Messiah. God fulfilled His promise through Joseph because he was in David's family line. Had Jesus been adopted by anyone else the scripture wouldn't have been fulfilled.

Old Testament prophesy also declared that Jesus would be born in the city of Bethlehem, Joseph's hometown. God predestined Joseph to fulfill the earthly role as Jesus' father before the first man or woman walked the earth. This was God's intent, not a backup plan.

I wholeheartedly believe that God intended for Joshua to be my son. I received two calls regarding potential adoptions that failed to come to fruition because God didn't ordain them, but the journey brought me to the child God saved for me.

I listened when God said, "Joshua Michael is your son." When God spoke, fear, anxiety, and worry were replaced with peace, love, and joy.

And just like Joseph, I didn't waste any time following God's plans for our lives.

Another similarity in our stories is that they both prove that you don't have to be rich to adopt. There's a myth that to adopt, a person must have a lot of money. I'll attempt to dispel it.

Joseph was a carpenter. He didn't have a lot of money to bestow on Jesus, but what he had was more important. Joseph gave Jesus the gifts of a safe home, Old Testament teachings, and unconditional love. God didn't predestine Joseph to parent Jesus because he was rich; his obedience, integrity, and faith were more important.

The fact that Jesus was born in a stable was no accident. It was part of the divine plan. God wanted to show the world that Jesus came to save everyone from their sins, not just the wealthy.

As a single mother, I knew adoption wouldn't be easy, emotionally or financially. I embraced every bit of it because I wanted to share God's blessings with a child of my own.

I was raised in the SE quadrant of Washington, DC, one of the most underserved areas of the city. Depending upon the metric, that section of the city has either the highest or the lowest statistics. Thankfully, my parents raised us to embrace faith, family, love, and education and to have strong work ethics. We were middle-class and appreciated everything our parents worked to provide. This is the strong similarity between the earthly father that God chose for Joseph and the mother He chose for Joshua. We both honored God through obedience and love. He doesn't emphasize the importance of earthly riches, but rather inner qualities. I thank God for selecting me. Becoming a mother enriched my life. Not through money, but in love and memories. Worldly possessions mean nothing without the love of family.

Oftentimes, people equate adoption with longing, loss, and despair. The news Mary gave Joseph was a pretty tough pill to swallow, wasn't it? He was so upset he was going to break up with her. I'm sure grief and sadness almost derailed him as he considered how to handle the situation. Back then, Mary could've been stoned to death for being unfaithful.

Can you imagine seeing the woman you love dying that type of death?

Once Joseph heard from the angel of God for himself, he obeyed, followed instructions, and turned his grief into action. Eventually, his despair melted into love.

Growing together with Joshua has been one of the most exhilarating experiences of my life. It hasn't been without its hiccups, though. Sometimes, shades of abandonment creep up out of nowhere. My heart aches when my son asks, "Why did my mother give me up?" or "Do you know where my father is?"

These questions nearly break me, but I remain strong for my child.

Life isn't always happy, but I remind Joshua of our blessings. As we discuss the God we serve, I urge him to remember that God doesn't make mistakes.

Isaiah 61:3 tells us that God will give us *"a crown of beauty instead of ashes"*. Sadness, grief, and despair aren't intended to hang around. God heals and restores us. In Him, we find joy and purpose.

Chapter 9
The Lessons Learned

Motherhood is the most important role that I'll ever fulfill in my life. Parents take care of each of their children's needs in addition to their own. Instilling values and principles isn't an easy thing; children watch what we do more than listen to what we say. We have to live by the principles we're trying to impart.

Parenthood is filled with peaks and valleys. It takes patience to get through the valleys, that's why God ensured that my muscle grew strong enough to handle the rough days. Even as I typed this manuscript, my son provided proof that patience is needed to nurture and love.

There are a few lessons that I learned from the Pharoah's daughter and Joseph. Although I'm not raising baby Jesus or Moses, I am raising a child of God.

Joseph teaches us to trust God even when it doesn't make any sense.

I'm sure many people thought adopting a baby as a single mother wasn't the brightest idea in the world, nor would it be the easiest. Packing the two of us up to leave the house was a task. But where there's a will, I'm determined to figure out a way. And that's exactly what I did.

Another lesson learned was not to give up hope during the wait. There's always something that we can improve, grow or enjoy in our lives. In the meantime, don't focus on what you're waiting for. Trust God with all your heart and remember that He won't leave you. There are always classes that you can take to learn a new talent or engage with friends. Engage family members and friends who feed you positive thoughts.

Once we receive the desires of our heart, there will be days when we ask ourselves, "Really? Is this what I prayed for?" Sometimes, you may think your best isn't good enough, but don't give up. Galatians 6:9 says, *"Let us not become weary in doing good, for at the proper time we will reap a harvest if we don't give up."* Even if we don't reap the harvest, future generations may because the scripture says, "…at the right time."

Do your best while you're on your journey. That's what's asked of us. No one is perfect. God gives us grace, but we have to remember to extend grace to ourselves and others, too.

Love covers a multitude of sins. Displaying unconditional love helps us walk away from some offenses. Be the first to say, "I'm sorry." Tell them, "I love you," during the hard times. It takes strength to move beyond your hurt and pain. God prepared us for the moment … during the wait.

Chapter 10

The Encouragement

Thank you for reading my first non-fiction work. I hope you are encouraged to step out on faith and receive everything God has for you. Build your fortitude because God has heard your prayers. *"So you also must be ready, because the Son of Man will come at an hour when you do not expect Him."* (Matthew 24:44). In other words, stay ready so you don't have to get ready.

If the thought of adoption has ever crossed your mind, I'd like you to consider that it may've been the voice of God tugging at your heart. If this book cover caught your eye, that may've been God speaking to you, as well. Nothing compares to motherhood, the most important role I'll ever have in my lifetime.

Typically, there are three reasons why people don't adopt: the cost, paperwork, and sheer intimidation. The thing about women; however, is when we want something, we move everything out of our way. While we're working, God is clearing the path for us.

If you've ever felt the pull on your heartstring to adopt, I'd encourage you to pursue it. It's one of the most Christ-like things that anyone can do in their lives and will fill your heart with joy.

If God is calling you to adopt, to go someplace, or to give something … patience will lead you through the process. And you won't fail to persevere.

Terri Ann Johnson

is an award-winning, author for her debut novel, Faith Alone, which has been optioned for a movie. She writes books with hope exploding from the pages through tragedy, adversity, and triumph. The national bestselling author expertly spotlights everyday people embroiled in not-so-ordinary circumstances with wisdom and compassion; her focus on faith, forgiveness, and restoration not only allows readers to get lost between the pages but be inspired by them.

To learn more please visit her website,
www.TerriAnnJohnson.com
Sociatap: http://bit.ly/TAJSociaTap
Email: terrijohnson419@gmail.com

The Merry Hearts Inspirational Series will warm your heart and touch your soul . . .

Faith Alone is based in D C. and it's the story of 42-year-old Lachelle Jackson who's living her best life. She's in a happy marriage and loves her job, but then discovers that she's facing a life-threatening pregnancy. In the midst of that. . . a strategy occurs. In Faith Alone we watch Lachelle lean on her faith while navigating life's storms.

Faith Alone

Chapter One

I gripped the pregnancy box in my hand, thinking that telling my husband that I might be pregnant should be one of the most exciting days of my life. Keyword: should. I had buried any and all thoughts of motherhood forever.

The sound of my heart beating hammered in my ears. Lying on the couch didn't comfort me. So still holding onto the box, I got up and walked into the kitchen, and headed straight to the fridge; but I couldn't eat.

I tried to think: what would I normally be doing while I waited for Brian to come home? Then, I shook that thought away. It didn't matter at this point because there wouldn't be anything normal about the conversation Brian and I would have once he walked through the door.

Part of me thought that maybe I would take care of this by myself, without ever telling him, without him finding out. But I learned in my younger years that lies could equal loss. The last thing I wanted to lose was Brian. So it was best for me to honor my vows, best for me to handle this, for better or for worse.

And this part was the worst.

I glanced down at the box and set it in the middle of the dining room table.

He'll see it there, that's for sure.

Then, I staggered back into the living room. But not a second later, a car door slammed, and I jumped up off the couch, stubbing my baby toe on the edge of the coffee table. Dayum. Dayum. Dayum.

The pain didn't stop me, though. I raced down the hallway into the dining room, slipping on our polished hardwood floors, but thank God, I didn't fall.

I grabbed the pregnancy test from the table, then dashed up the stairs. Breathing hard, I hid it in our bathroom, tossing it onto the vanity. Then, I took a couple of moments to get settled.

Once my breathing was back to normal, I moseyed down the stairs, a stark contrast to the crazy woman who'd been running around the house a few minutes ago.

Telling him is the best way.

That was what I'd decided. Brian wouldn't play games with me by leaving information sitting on the table, so I didn't want to do that to him. I would tell Brian what I knew: that I was two weeks late for my period and because I'd been so focused on meeting the deadline for the grant I'd just submitted, I hadn't noticed my missed period until this morning.

I had it all worked out in my mind; I knew exactly how we would handle this. But Brian was a problem-solver. Would my husband try to fix this? Or would he go along with my plan?

By the time I reached the bottom of the stairs, I was surprised that Brian still had not come through the door. I curled up on the leather sectional, pulling my favorite, fuzzy throw blanket over my legs, wanting my husband to find me in my most relaxed state.

Still, no Brian. What was taking him so long? I pushed myself off the couch and peeked out the window. Brian's car wasn't even in the driveway. It must have been a neighbor that I'd heard.

Get it together, Lachelle.

Returning to the sofa, I grabbed the latest edition of O Magazine and tried to focus on Suzie Orman's article, but my thoughts soon wandered. Maybe if I practiced, my words would come out with more confidence. Maybe if I practiced, I wouldn't scare my husband to death.

Taking a breath, I said, "Brian, I have something to tell you." I imagined how I would sit him down, grab his hands and say, "Brian, I'm pregnant."

I practiced those two sentences over and over until it felt ridiculous and then, I turned on the TV. The news droned on and on until the anchor said, "Now, turning to local news, another young girl has been reported missing, here in D.C."

A picture of a girl, no more than thirteen or fourteen, flashed on the screen and I turned the TV off before the anchor could say the girl's name. That was certainly not something I wanted to hear right now.

Before I could find another distraction, I heard the slam of another car door. I froze, though I still wasn't sure if it was Brian until, "Are you working on your rebound, Matt?" my husband asked our teenage neighbor. There was a pause, and then, his voice again. "Yeah, okay, meet me at the gym around noon tomorrow."

I began counting the seconds from him locking the car to walking up the six steps to checking the mailbox. His keys jingled as he opened the door, and I was still frozen in place on the sofa.

One, two, three, "Chellllllllllle, I'm home."

Once he turned the corner and saw me lying on the couch, he belted out, "I don't see nothing wrong with a little bump and grind." Brian wiggled his non-rhythmic hips and began moving toward me as though his alter ego's name was B-Fine, because he was fine, all five feet and nine inches of him. He'd played college football, and the girls used to flirt with him, telling him that he looked like Emmitt Smith. It was true; it was his smile and his complexion.

But although he could run that ball, he could never really dance. Usually, if a guy couldn't dance, I would never let him get past first base. Why waste my time? But Brian was so fine and sweet, and once we became more than friends, he squashed my myth. He proved that just because you didn't have rhythm on your feet, didn't mean you didn't know what to do between the sheets.

I forced a smile as he fumbled with the buttons on his shirt.

"Alexa," he called out to our Echo, "put on R. Kelly's Bump and Grind." The whole time, his eyes remained on me. Brian couldn't get those cufflinks off to save his life, but he didn't care. His goofiness and pretend ineptness was all part of the fun. Then, he crouched down, got on his hands and knees, and crawled the rest of the way to the couch.

But right before he reached me, he shouted, "Ouch." He picked through the carpet, then held up the pushpin that had stabbed his hand.

I couldn't help but laugh. "Luckily, you only strip for me, babe. Come here and let mama kiss da boo boo."

"Alexa, turn it off. My entertainment for this evening is done." Brian took his shoes off and laid down with me.

We loved this couch. It held the two of us comfortably. I snuggled under his chin. This was my sweet spot.

After a few moments, he said, "Usually my striptease act cracks you up. You okay?"

I should've known that he'd noticed a difference in my demeanor.

"I'm okay," I lied.

"Are you hungry? Were you waiting for me to eat? It's so nice outside; I should throw a few things on the grill."

Dinner. "Uhmmm, I hadn't really thought about food." I wished the world would stop right here, right now.

"Well, I know a nice, chargrilled steak will put you in the right mood. Let me get up and thaw out two rib-eyes. Can you take out the ingredients for my sauce while I run upstairs?"

As he rolled away from me and sat up, I shouted out, "Brian, I'm pregnant."

I couldn't hold it in any longer. "I'm about two weeks late." Then, I spilled out the rest of the story in one long breath, "I was working so hard on that grant submission for Loving Our Babies that I didn't even think about it until this morning. I stopped at the drug store on my way home and picked up a pregnancy test so that we could take it this evening. I knew that you would want to be with me."

His eyes were wide and then, he motioned with his hands. "Chelle, slow down." He shook his head when he said, "So, you don't know that you're pregnant, right? As much birth control as we use, could it really happen?"

I gave him a side-eye. "As much sex as we have, I guess so."

He exhaled a long breath as if he could blow this challenge away. "Well, let's not assume anything. The stress of your job may've contributed to you being late."

As I looked up, directly into his face, I said, "You know I'm never late. I've been stressing about telling you all day."

His silence told me that he was thinking, thinking of a way to fix this.

I sat up and twisted because I wanted to look into his eyes when I whispered, "There's nothing you can do to fix this. It was a mistake. Let's just correct it."

He took another deep breath, then another long exhale before he pushed himself off the couch and picked up his shirt. The way he leaned against the wall and rubbed his eyes, I knew he was thinking, thinking, thinking.

Then after what felt like too many seconds, he said in the most respectful tone, "It wasn't a mistake. This was God's plan." He slipped back into his shirt, then walked over and knelt in front of me. "What happened to you happened almost twenty-five years ago. Doctors know more now and medical technology has advanced."

I shook my head. "But I could die," I said through my tears. "I am forty-two years old," I added like I needed to remind him of all the facts. "I have a history of high blood pressure and I had a baby that…"

He didn't let me finish. "Look at me." His voice was so gentle, so full of love. His touch was the same as he wiped my tears, then tilted my chin upward. "No one is dying, no one. Let's take this step by step. We'll take the test tonight and we'll call Doctor Price in the morning. Is that a plan?"

He spoke so assuredly that all I could say was, "Yes."

"My Chelle, you married a man, a man who will stand with you through the storms of life. We have each other and God is on our side."

Brian wiped more of my tears away and moved my natural curls out of my face. When he kissed me, I really thought that everything in my world would now be all right.

Keyword: *thought*.

http://bit.ly/FaithAloneEbook

COMING WINTER 2021

After a tragedy occurs, Lachelle slowly begins to heal and focus on raising her baby daughter until her high school sweetheart John resurfaces in her life and they rekindle their love. News exposes, that their son, who they thought had died at childbirth twenty-years earlier may be alive. This new information includes a scheme that could reveal secrets that will leave Lachelle and John caught up in drama and intrigue. Will this destroy their new beginning and sabotage their happily ever after?

Switched

Chapter One

"Today was a good day." Ice Cube's vibrato bounced through the speakers of my SUV as I watched Lachelle enter the lobby of her ten-story condominium. Once she stepped inside and waved bye, I gave her the peace sign and hit the gas pedal. The windshield wipers automatically cleaned the early morning dew from the glass. Even though Ice Cube's declaration was in the past tense, I felt that I'd have a good day and it was only nine-thirty in the morning.

Today marked what would've been the twenty-fourth birthday of our son, Christian. Gravesite visits were my way of atoning for not being present on the day of his birth which was also the day of his death. Visiting his grave was the least I could do.

But this year was different. Christian's mother, Lachelle, and I visited together. We were high school sweethearts who lost touch after our baby was born, still. I shouldn't even say lost touch. That was a cop-out. I needed to re-phrase. I left for my first year of college. And after my mother told me that Lachelle lost our baby, I wasn't mature enough to come home and check on her. But I never stopped thinking about her. I'd never forget the first day we met.

February 10, 1993

Southern High School. The instant I left my coach's office, disappointment and fear walked me and my Air Force Ones to the library. I felt as though I let myself and down. And I feared what my mother would do to me if I got kicked off the team. Basketball was my life.

I could still hear Coach Richard's ultimatum. "Raise that GPA or sit out next season. I won't jeopardize this program when you can't keep your grades up."

I never liked to study. Most of my teachers were women and I'd always used my classroom leadership abilities and personality to move my final grades up a notch. Sophomore year hadn't been the easiest and my C average grades dipped to a low D. Coach wasn't happy. As much as I didn't want to take his recommendation, I didn't have any other options if I wanted to play ball.

"I've set you up with a tutor. His name is on the paper." He shoved it across his desk.

I grabbed the note and shrieked. "Coach, I'm not trying to be tutored by this little geek. The team loves jonin' and I'll have to leave school over this."

Coach stood up and rounded the corner of his workspace. "If you don't get those grades up, your mother will find out and her foot will be so far up your tail that you won't have to worry about the team."

Unfortunately, he was right. If I really wanted to play, get a basketball scholarship to college and keep my mom's foot outta my butt, then I needed to get this tutoring session started and bring my grades up.

I entered the library and noticed a few pairs of tutoring teams. But I didn't see the boy genius that was supposed to turn me into a sudden Trigonometry wiz.

"Excuse me, do you know where I can find Sherman Duckett? I'm here for a tutoring session."

The librarian turned from stacking books and responded, "He's no longer a tutor. Lachelle Williams has replaced him." She gestured her arm toward the window. "She's over there."

Love at first sight and I were strangers. But on this day, not only did we meet...we became best friends. I wasn't sure what I expected a tutor to look like, but it wasn't what I saw.

All of a sudden, my stomach felt queasy, and I wondered if she could hear my heart beating, although there were at least twenty steps between us.

Lachelle sat under a window as the sun's rays shined on her radiant mocha brown complexion. She gave off an air of intelligence with the tip of her pencil wedged between her teeth. A frown of concentration washed across her face as she twisted her mouth to the side. She snatched the pencil from her mouth and erased something on the paper as though she didn't want any reminder of what was previously there.

Still standing at the librarian's desk, I checked her out. Since the shorter side of her asymmetric bob faced me, I saw her bamboo earring swinging on her neck. The serious look on her face told me that I needed to step to her correct.

The hushed laughter of students broke her spell and she looked up and back down.

Wait? She didn't even notice me?

So, I strutted straight over to the light oak rectangle library table.

Keep your cool John.

Once I was standing in front of her, she switched her focus from her notes to me. As hard as I tried to play it cool, my mouth betrayed me.

"What's up, shawty?" slipped out.

That was not how I wanted my introduction to go. She was not the type of girl who you called a shawty. The hint of sophistication was what attracted me to her.

Recover John, recover.

People always thought that athletes were just jocks who only focused on playing sports and nothing else. But that wasn't me and that wasn't the image I wanted to portray. It was bad enough that I was coming to Lachelle for tutoring. But I couldn't have this pretty lady thinking that I was some dumb jock, naw, I'd present myself better than that.

I held out my hand and she shook it. "I'm John, John Braxton. I believe I'm meeting you for a tutoring session."

She looked me up and down and didn't seem, at all, impressed.

"Are you Lachelle Williams?"

Once her almond-shaped eyes met mine, she responded. "I am." She shook my hand. "And you, Mr. Braxton, are five minutes late."

I wanted to say, 'Well that's because I didn't know that I was meeting with a fine tutor.' But I didn't.

The empty wooden chair next to her scraped against the floor as I pulled it out. But my attention stayed laser-focused on miss lady.

At six feet, seven inches, fitting my legs under this table was awkward.

She watched me stretch my legs and cross them under the table. My height was a blessing and a curse. If girls weren't attracted to you because you played basketball, they'd say something stupid like, 'I can't see myself having to stand on my tippy toes to kiss my boyfriend'.

Although Lachelle was sitting down and I couldn't see her legs, her torso was long with a little meat on her, which I liked.

"Yeah, I'm a little late. Coach called me to his office, and I got here as soon as I could." I leaned forward. "I'm surprised that we've never met before. You're a Junior, right?" I wanted to get to know everything that I could about her.

"I am. But I'm in the honors program so we wouldn't get a chance to see each other." She shifted in her seat, and a devilish smile crept across her lips.

I laid my right hand across my heart as though she'd just stabbed me with a dagger. "Miss Tutor, don't be so mean." I reached over to my backpack, which I'd laid in the chair next to me, and pulled out my Trigonometry book, placing it on the table. "Trig is killing me."

"Well, I guess we should set a schedule," Lachelle grabbed a pen from her purse. "And you have to be here on time because I have my own studying to do."

I lived by routine. So that wouldn't be any problem.

"Can we make a deal?"

She nodded. "I hope that I don't regret agreeing to this deal."

I laughed out loud. "Naw, I gotchu. It'll be, what they say, a win-win?"

She flipped the pages in her day-timer. Her eyebrows shifted upward; interest spilled from her lips. "And what do I win?"

I sensed a competitive spirit that pulled me in even more. My life was all about the contest and shawty wasn't afraid to spar a little. But I thought that I'd slow things down, just a little. I didn't want her to think that I was pressed, even though I was.

"I'll think of something. Let's go over the schedule. "I have a test next week and I'd like to set up a time to go over my notes."

Look at me, sounding scholarly.

Lachelle didn't look up from her planner. "Do you have practice on Thursdays?"

"Actually, I don't."

She nodded. "Great let's try to meet at three-thirty.

I packed my things and proceeded to get up. I hadn't forgotten about our bet, but I wanted to gauge her level of interest. When I came in she acted as though I didn't exist up in this school.

Lachelle huffed and folded her arms over her chest. "So, what about the bet?"

"Oh yeah," I responded as though I forgot. "I thought of something that definitely will be a win-win!"

She nodded. "I hope that I don't regret agreeing to this 'win-win'."

"Naw, I gotchu." Moving the chair that I sat in out of the way, I leaned against the table, crossing my arms over my chest. "Well, if I end the school year with a C or better in math then we go to the movies together."

She arched her eyebrows before responding. "And if you don't...?"

"Oh, I'll win. Trust me. I've worked hard to accomplish goals all of my life." I flashed my pearly whites. "Very seldom do I lose."

She raised those eyebrows, again, as though she didn't believe me.

"It's a bet," she responded. A school-girl giggle escaped from her throat. At that moment I thought…she just might like me.

My chest swelled with hope.

My cell phone rang through the speakers, snapping me back to the present and diverting my attention to the dashboard. It was Smitty, my agent, probably calling to press me about the ESPN interview on Monday morning. That brotha could be worse than a nagging woman.

I pressed the green phone button on the dash.

"What's up, Smitty?"

William Smith and I met in our freshman year at Kentucky. I was the athlete, and he was the scholar. Growing up, you attracted girls in one of two ways: athletics or academics. Smitty kept it real. He knew he'd never get girls by balling. He stayed on the Dean's list. He was an average-looking dude with an average sense of humor. He set his sights on earning his law degree to get the attention of the ladies, and he succeeded. I was a city boy and he hailed from the South, but we've been tight since we met.

"My man, fifty grand." Smitty's southern drawl echoed through the truck as I bolted through the yellow light five minutes from home. "Did you handle your business this morning?"

Smitty wouldn't go straight into the business of the day, the real reason he called. But it was coming soon.

"I made my annual pilgrimage. But Lachelle and I went together. It was a good visit."

"Yo bruh, you smash yet?"

Smitty's filter was nonexistent. "Bruh, I'm really into her, don't ask me that. And besides, we're Christians."

He was quiet for a moment. I knew that meant trouble. He finally responded. "Don't Christians smash?"

Pushing the red phone button on the dashboard to end this conversation should've been my next move. Smitty knew the closeness that grew between Lachelle and me over the past year. He should've known better than to describe intimacy between her and me as smashing. What was going on with us was serious. After twenty-four years, Lachelle and I both had our own baggage, but we were lightening our loads. I was feeling her, and she was feeling me.

People thought luck brought Lachelle and me together at Christian's gravesite a year ago today. But I knew it was divine intervention, combined with a little assistance from her best friend, Tracy.

But instead of cutting Smitty off, I waved at the guard as I entered my gated community and continued talking. "Dude, just tell me what you want? I'm walking into the house now. I'd like to shave, and shower, then grab some grub before I leave for New York."

Even though I was only pulling up to the crib, I needed to tell that little white lie so that I could hurry him off the phone.

"So, you're ready? Packed and everything? We're meeting a few of the ESPN head honchos tonight for dinner. It'll be a non-interview, interview."

This was the epitome of our friendship, Smitty watered everything down for me as though I needed help understanding.

"Yes. You've told me that, a few times. And before you ask, I have the itinerary and the tickets that your assistant sent."

"Okay, dude. I'll let you go get to it," he responded.

After removing the audio from the blue tooth, I pulled the phone to my ear.

"I'll get wit' you later."

Smitty ended the call with his customary sign-off, "Holla back."

The first time I saw this twenty-floor upscale apartment building I knew I'd make it my home. The plethora of diverse restaurants, two entertainment centers, and high-end shops sitting alongside cobblestone sidewalks was the new place to be in the city. I pulled my key fob out of the glove box, entered, and parked in my designated parking space. I jumped out, locked the truck, and accessed the elevator taking me straight to my apartment.

"Hel-lo." This was one of my habits of coming into an empty house and announcing my entrance. The echo bounced through the one thousand square foot space. Moving boxes still lined the walls, as I'd only been here for about a month. If I was gonna live between DC and NYC this vibrant area was my choice. My dream job was in the Big Apple, but the woman of my dreams lived in the Nation's Capital.

But first things first, I wanted this gig. ESPN approached me to work as a sports analyst/commentator. Talking about the game of basketball... heaven.

I grabbed an apple out of the fridge and ran up the stairs to the master bedroom where the view overlooked the Potomac River. God blessed me with a skill and a career that not only allowed me to have this kind of home but to travel with my work. Determining where to retire wasn't a hard decision. Hope, my twelve-year-old daughter, lived in the suburbs of Washington, DC with my ex-wife, Dayna. Bonding with Hope was the major reason I'd settled here.

I had other reasons, too – Lachelle and her baby girl, Faith. But again, first things first.

The Acela train rolled out of Union Station at twelve twenty this afternoon. I'd make it there on time, but I needed to get moving.

I always hated a quiet house, so I turned on the TV and the local news blared.

After showering, I walked into the closet and pulled out a pair of comfortable khakis and a polo shirt. They'd do. I grabbed my socks, undershirt, and underwear from my drawer and sat down on the edge of my bed. The music that accompanied the breaking news segments caught my attention.

A news story had been circulating about switched babies at a local hospital. I'd caught the tail end of it a few times. But today a date that the reporter mentioned caused me to pay attention.

"This, allegedly, took place during May through July in 1993. It has not been reported how many babies were switched but as one family stated, 'even one baby is too many.' There are reports of bribery from families to switch infants due to known illnesses of their babies."

The shirt that I was about to throw over my head dropped to the floor.

Summer 1993.

Stunned, I sat on the edge of the bed. Christian was born at Sibley Hospital during the summer of 1993, but I needed to confirm the particular hospital with Lachelle because maybe I was trippin'.

Before I picked up the phone, I snatched the remote off the pillow next to me, hit the rewind button, then replayed the segment.

Summer 1993. Sibley Hospital. Baby switching.

I couldn't call her; she'd detect the worry in my voice. I grabbed my cell and sent her a simple text to ask her a simple question.

Where was Christian born?

The answer might prove to alter the trajectory of our lives.

Scooping my shirt from the floor, I tossed it over my head. I had to focus and get ready to catch this train. I was probably making something up in my head. I leaned over and glanced at the phone's screen to ensure that I didn't miss her text.

Nothing.

As I rubbed the oil on my hands to run over my hair, I heard Lachelle's designated ring tone. Reaching for the phone, I knocked the oil over onto the nightstand. The bath towel was within my reach, but I grabbed the phone first. I'd clean the oil up later.

"Hey babe," I said picked up the towel, and cleaned the oil from the hardwood floor. "You could've responded with a text," I teased.

"I wanted to hear your voice, that way I can glean your disposition." After a beat of silence, she asked, "Why'd you ask me about the hospital?"

I knew where this conversation was headed based on the sound of her voice.

"Have you heard about the baby switching shenanigans at Sibley Hospital?"

"I have, but wasn't it recent?"

"Well, I just heard the summer of 1993."

Lachelle let out a heavy sigh. "Christian was born at Sibley."

Thoughts flooded my mind and the first prominent one was to go to Sibley, right now, and demand answers.

"I can't go to New York, not today. I need to know if our child was caught up in this scheme...I need - "

"John, slow down. I want answers too. But nothing will change between today and when you return. You'll be back tomorrow evening."

I knew she was right, but I didn't let up. "I can't focus on this interview."

"You will focus on the interview because it's your dream. We'll talk and develop a game plan when you return."

I flopped down on the bed, without responding.

Lachelle's voice reassured me that my thoughts were irrational. "John, marching up there demanding an answer will only prove to get you thrown out. And it may scare them into hiding information even deeper...if there's anything to hide."

If there's anything to hide?

"You don't believe that this could be true?" I asked.

"I'm saying let's work as a team and develop a game plan to finding out." Her voice softened which caused me to consider her request. "You know the importance of a good game plan."

"You're right. I'll be back on Saturday evening. We'll talk about the next steps then." While Lachelle didn't seem to have the urgency that I exhibited I knew once she said something, her word was her bond.

"Okay, now get out of there before you miss the train."

"I love you soon to be Mrs. Braxton."

"And I love you too, Mr. Braxton."

We ended our call, and I went into the bathroom to throw a few things in my bag. Looking into the mirror I asked myself, "Did we just visit our son or someone else's?"

Following a successful undercover FBI sting operation that took more out of him than he could ever imagine, Agent Mateo Lopez is disillusioned and uncertain if it's time to cash out and retire. A confirmed workaholic, his career soared at the cost of his love life which had crashed and burned until mutual friends arranged a date with Rachel Jordan who manages a children's social service agency. Unlucky in love, Rachel has sworn off romantic relationships.

Mateo finds himself falling for the sharp-witted Rachel and one of her new cases raises red flags. She's sucked into danger and doesn't even know it. He'll do everything in his power to keep her and the children safe even if it means resorting to extreme measures.

Will the choices they make cost them their lives or bring them closer together?

Knight of Penn Quarter

Chapter One

Agent Mateo Lopez, known as "El Gato", the cat with many lives, decided that neither curiosity nor his career with the FBI would be his cause of death.

Despite telling the agency that he was done, here he sat as his supervisor, Janice Clark, poured over his personnel service record planning to send him into danger yet again.

"You're an accomplished agent and I see why your code name is The Cat, the man with many lives. I can't imagine it's your intent to give up your outstanding career at this point."

"Intent?" His throaty sounds mimicked laughter, except it left a bad taste in his mouth and was tinged with bitterness. "If a man is lucky to escape one close call after another, he has a chance to think about things and it was never my intent to be in my grave before the age of thirty-five."

He should've walked straight to Human Resources and turned in his early retirement papers after his last FBI undercover operation went terribly wrong. He was done with everything and his blood boiled as he sat in Agent Clark's office.

"It's been a long morning already," she said. "I think I'll have a cup while we discuss this matter."

Observing her deliberate attempts to placate him as she stood and walked over to the Keurig, he knitted his brow and sighed while she took her time searching through the different flavors of coffee and finally inserted a pod into the machine.

"Agent Lopez, I'll need you on this one."

Undeterred in his decision to get out of the office as soon as possible, he observed her while she stood in front of the coffeemaker. As it gurgled, she smiled and inhaled the aroma of the strong brew filling the air.

"I'd like to give you more high-profile assignments."

"More cases? Sounds interesting, Agent Clark, but as I said, I'm done."

"Hear me out. I can make sure the assignments are in exotic locations so that you can mix business and pleasure." Wiggling her eyebrows, she gave him a sly, all-knowing smile.

Mateo's ten-year career with the FBI had its ups and downs, but the last operation rocked him to the core.

"After everything, even that carrot doesn't appeal to me and besides, it's time for me to do my own thing."

"I know you still have bad feelings about the last operation— "

"Bad feelings," he shot back. "Is that what you're calling it?"

She sat behind the huge mahogany desk which swallowed her petite frame. At five feet and two inches tall, she often kept her blond hair tied in a tall bun on top of her head to add an additional inch to her height. She was probably in her mid-sixties but didn't look a day over fifty-five. She knew her stuff and slinging back at others when needed, she took as much as she gave. Understanding the old boy mentality that still operated throughout the agency, she knew how to play the game; most of the times, she got what she wanted.

"You still haven't heard me out."

"I'm listening Agent Clark." Studying her with a laser focus, he wondered about her intent.

Two years had passed since a dirty agent had accused Mateo of teaming up with the Sanchez drug cartel in Mexico and setting their ground operation on fire to get rid of evidence. It's the same drug cartel which was responsible for importing a huge amount of cocaine and guns into the United States for at least five years. Mateo was the first agent the FBI was able to use to infiltrate the organization and get information that could incriminate them. Unfortunately, once the real rat, Agent Fletcher, accused Mateo of conspiring with the enemy, he'd been arrested and charged, spending a day in jail until his arraignment.

Anger tap-danced on the outskirts of his mind as he thought of the toll being arrested and wrongly accused took on him and his family. If it wasn't for Carlos Rivera, his lawyer, and a lifelong friend at the DEA, who had also infiltrated the organization and provided the proof of his innocence, he might still be behind bars.

The spirit of El Gato was destroyed by this agency. He died waiting in that jail like a common criminal. He frowned and her voice brought him out of his thoughts.

"You know we dismissed Agent Fletcher after lying about what happened on the op."

"That's the least that should've happened." Mateo leaned back in his chair and unbuttoned his jacket.

"Why me? I've been training the recruits since then and I'm not trying to go back out in the field." Mateo reached into his wallet, pulled out one of his business cards, and offered it to her. "Everyone in this unit has heard me talking about my company, Global Connections Security. I'm ready to get back out there, but this time, on my terms and with a crew, I can trust."

Mateo didn't care how she took the news as he shared what had been on his mind for a long time.

In her silence, he continued, "I've been loyal to the FBI for years, played by the books, and still, I was arrested as if I couldn't be trusted. I'm curious as to why you want someone that you don't trust to continue working for you?" He crossed his legs and waited for her answer.

"I had your back every step of the way," she replied. "This entire department did. And yes, I'm asking you to come back because you still have a lot to offer. You're one of my best agents."

"I couldn't tell," Mateo huffed.

The undercover assignments had wreaked havoc on Mateo's personal life. Witnessing small crimes and letting them go in an effort to accomplish the larger goal. Getting caught in one crisis after another, often knowing that it was by his own wits and survival skills that he made it out alive. As much as Mateo wanted to feel as though he was putting a dent in some of the illegal activities assigned to him, he ended up feeling as though he was paddling upstream in rough waters without an oar.

Yet, he had chosen this life and knew from the beginning that being undercover presented multiple issues that kept many agents single. In the undercover game, agents made enemies and he didn't want to fall in love with someone and cause them to become targets. So, he distanced himself from his blood family to keep them safe hoping they understood.

However, when it came to girlfriends, he had to be honest and accept that he loved the company of beautiful women who, too many times, used him for the perks of his job. They loved meeting him in exotic places where his assignments took him, the wining and dining in expensive restaurants as a part of his cover. They were misguided about the big government paycheck they thought agents received, without realizing that they were public servants and not rolling in cash. Mateo had trust issues and he made it clear to them ensuring they understood anything they did as a couple wasn't serious, just fun.

"I know that the last op caused you pain, in more ways than one," Agent Clark insisted. "But you were trained and experienced enough to deal with the pressure."

"Facts." Mateo nodded, but he was burned out and wanted to run his own company. His full-time job interfered with his dream.

Mateo recalled the time when he was first approached to work on the Sanchez Cartel operation. They needed someone with his background and knowledge of San Miguel de Allende, Mexico, where his parents were born and only twelve hours from Laredo, Texas. He'd only visited a few times as a child and saw it as an opportunity to give back to his ancestral home and reconnect with old friends like the Rivera family who now lived one hundred and seventy miles away in Mexico City. He felt certain that after so many years, no one there would recognize him as a grown man. Because he was skilled as an agent and had thorough knowledge of the people and their customs, he was assigned the lead instead of Agent Fletcher who was senior to him.

Agent Fletcher had done everything he could to ensure that it wasn't a success.

Mateo shifted in his seat as he verbalized his thoughts about the man, he believed was a trusted colleague, but who turned out to be his chief nemesis.

"Trust me, he won't get a job as a dog catcher in this country." She folded her hands on her desk and leaned in. "We've made sure of that."

At this point, Mateo brushed away his disappointment by working with the recruits which gave him the opportunity to touch a new generation and pour into their spirits the character of a real agent. Maybe that was what Agent Fletcher had been sorely missing.

"What is it that you need from me and what exactly are you asking?"

Her hazel eyes widened as she sipped her coffee.

"We've gotten wind that there's an illegal operation involving a child services agency in the city. They're using foster kids to run drugs for them. They pay the foster parents extra money as an incentive.

Unfortunately, there are also allegations of sex trafficking."

News like that made Mateo recall some of his bleakest times as an agent. "And you want me to go in and do what?"

Agent Clark pulled a folder from her desk and opened it. "This is the man who we believe is responsible for the connection between the criminal enterprise and the Loving Our Babies Social Services Agency." She slid a picture across her desk to him.

Mateo peered at the black and white glossy photo and thought he may have recognized the face, but he was uncertain where they may have met. "Again, what are you asking me to do?"

"We'd like you to bring them down. Everything we know about the operation is in here."

He took the folder and eased out of the chair.

"I've spent twenty minutes longer in here than I intended. Thanks for the information but I'm not promising I'll do anything with it." Smiling, he turned toward the door.

"Think about it and let me know," she shot back clearly unmoved by anything he said.

"I'm headed to Human Resources to submit my early retirement paperwork, Agent Clark."

"Even if you do that today, you still have forty-eight hours to rescind it."

"Sometimes in life, you have to follow your spirit and I only stayed this long to make sure that I got a portion of my pension."

Seeing that the conversation was over, she rose and watched as he walked away.

"You can't fault me for trying."

"I don't. Goodbye." He left the office and looked down the hallway at the entrance to the Human Resources office. He couldn't shake the image of the man in the folder while shivers coursing down his spine concerned him; which was never a good sign.

https://bit.ly/PennKnightAmazoneBook

Greg and Karen have found true love after years in empty marriages, but their children have no desire to blend into one, big, happy family. Meanwhile, the six siblings, who appear to dislike each other, have formed an alliance fueled by the respective exes, to disrupt what their parents thought would've been a happy union.

Just at the point the parents learn their kids are in cahoots to sabotage their love because they're more comfortable with their 'new' parents being apart, a near tragedy serves to put everyone in the household on notice when an emergency school lock-down forces the oldest teen to realize that there is more to lose than just time away from his mother and his homies.

This Can't Be Us

Chapter One

"When did you stop loving my mother?" Li'l Greg blurted out as his father began explaining the reason for our 'Come to Jesus' meeting with the entire family today.

After wiping his brow, Greg responded, "I just stated that I wanted us to begin on a positive note. But since you want to bring up old stuff, your mother and I have been divorced for over five years."

The Jenkins family finished brunch on a sunny Saturday morning. Karen fixed something that everyone would love - Belgian waffles, bacon, turkey sausage links, scrambled eggs, and cheese grits. The dynamics of their blended family were hard to maneuver, but the one thing they could all agree upon was a good meal. They didn't know that their parents planned a discussion, hoping to resolve some of their family challenges.

The kids, all six of them, seemed to work each other's nerves and their parents' too. A few of them didn't respect Greg and Karen's marriage. After one year, it was time to stop ignoring the issues. The weekends were the only time when they were guaranteed to be in the same house. Approaching such a tough issue when they were still eating was a prime time.

"And I won't discuss the issues that destroyed our marriage," Greg continued. "That's not the purpose of this meeting. If you want to know the details, you should take that up with her." Greg snatched up his glass of orange juice almost spilling some. He stormed into the spacious family room and plopped down on the leather couch.

Li'l Greg pushed back from the table; ten pairs of younger eyes following his progression as he joined his father in the family room. He dropped onto the ottoman across from Greg, leaned in elbows resting on his knees. "When can I divorce you?" he asked, as his chest puffed out.

Greg's hope seemed to disappear when his broad shoulders fell, his lips pressed in a disapproving line.

"You left, and now you want us to come over here and play Brady Bunch with y'all every weekend?" the teen snapped. "I'm not doing my mama like that."

As usual everyone, all the way down to the seven-year-old, let Li'l Greg spew his anger speaking for the crew; the only time they seemed united. The sole sound echoing in the family room was the rattle of the neighbor's lawnmower. Karen wasn't sure if her oncoming migraine was a result of early fall allergies or the disrespectful kids. Her vote was for the latter.

"It ain't nothing to do out here," he said, with a sweeping gesture of his lanky arm, "all the way out in the boondocks. It's like you're trying to change who you are. But we're still the same." He jabbed a finger in his chest. "You can't change me. You can't change us."

* * *

Some of the kids had left the table and were watching from the threshold. Li'l Greg pushed his muscular frame up from the ottoman which sat next to the credenza. Smiles of bliss gleamed from an eight-by-ten framed wedding day photo. After a year of marriage, Karen thought that they would've been past this stage in trying to blend a family from being accustomed to living with one parent in the city to having two parents in the 'burbs.

And just when Karen didn't think the man/child could go any further, a comment, which in her house growing up could've gotten her teeth knocked out, was blurted out of Li'l Greg's mouth and in his father's ear. "And she ain't my mother," gesturing in Karen's direction as though referring to some trick in the street.

Karen gripped the edge of the dining room table.

Greg lunged toward his son, screaming, "You're out of line." He pulled up short, mere inches from his son. "Get it straight, your mother stopped loving me, not the other way around. When will you understand that?" Greg's sudden movement wiped the smug look off his son's face. Her husband's jaw tightened so hard that Karen thought it would break; not a good sign.

Li'l Greg didn't respond. His expression went from arrogant to humble. Even though his towering stature meant he could've stared directly into his father's eyes, he wisely avoided his glare. He had been all mouth a few minutes earlier, but he wasn't that crazy.

Realizing this had gone from bad to worse, Karen jumped from the dining room table. For a split second, she thought twice about coming between the two of them. Instead, she settled on grabbing Greg's waist from behind. "Come on babe. Sit back down."

Greg's middle child, Ava, inched back to the dining room table, where their so-called 'family meeting' had begun, whipped out her cell and soon had her soft, brown eyes glued to the screen, scrolling through her phone.

When Karen angled to place herself between the two Gregs, Ava looked up to see who would make the first move and what the move would be, her eyes poised to type. At fourteen, she never said much, but that didn't mean she didn't have a voice. Karen was totally aware that the tween was her mother's spy. She only came over to the house so that she could provide information to Greg's ex since information about what happened under their roof always found its way into Nicole's ear and out of her mouth. If Karen received more than a "hi" or "bye" from Ava, that was a good day. Karen was a non-factor in Ava's life, and she made sure to show it at every point.

Karen's fifteen-year-old son, Jalen, stepped forward to speak but paused for a moment. He was what most people would consider a nerd, but the Black Lives Movement had given him a certain bravado that he'd never had. Ta-Nehisi Coates had replaced the science fiction on his bookshelf. Jalen removed the white earbuds from his ears, in what Karen thought would be an effort to defuse the stand-off. Instead, Jalen erupted with a surprising, "Ma, you like this dude. We don't have to."

Wait. What? This dude?

Counting to ten first, Karen didn't address his disrespect toward Greg, the man of the house. Because if it was a diversion, it worked. Greg turned his head away from his son and glared at hers. His face became a mask of confusion.

She'd talk to Jalen later and get him straight on the proper way to address his stepfather, but at least Greg wasn't about to stomp a hole in his own son.

Karen's ten-year-old, Tiffany, moved to the dining room and slid into a seat next to Ava in an effort to view her cell phone screen. Ava sucked her teeth and rolled her eyes at Tiffany who moved her chair away, but still at a vantage point to watch the drama. Greg's youngest daughter, eight-year-old Kennedy, pleaded, "Miss Karen, can I go and watch Nickelodeon?"

Karen put one finger to her mouth then whispered, "In a few minutes." She nodded and tipped back into the family room to sit next to her stepbrother, Michael.

Karen's seven-year-old, Michael, slumped on the couch blinking rapidly, a sure sign that he was worried. As he clutched an iPad to the John Wall jersey draped on his tiny frame, Karen moved from Greg's side to sit next to her youngest son, rubbing his back to let him know that everything would be alright, trying to convey a feeling that she couldn't manage herself.

Greg's stare bounced between Karen's son and his before he snatched his keys from the coffee table. "Karen, I'll be back."

"Wait." Karen tried to grab his arm before he stormed out of the house. Unfortunately, the only thing she caught was the smell of freshly mowed grass as the storm door slammed in her face. She pushed it open and yelled, "Where are you going?"

Greg jumped in his SUV. The passenger side window lowered. "I need some fresh air."

Karen needed the same.

The next thing she heard was the tires screeching as he sped up the street.

https://bit.ly/ThisCBeUs

www.ingramcontent.com/pod-product-compliance
Lightning Source LLC
Chambersburg PA
CBHW011318080526
44589CB00020B/2750